Ephrata Cloister

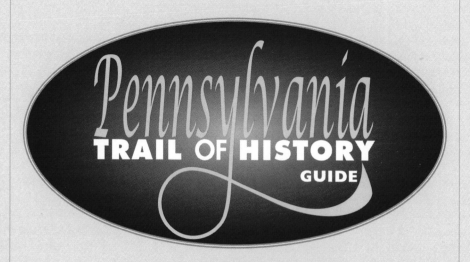

Text by John Bradley
Photographs by Craig A. Benner

STACKPOLE BOOKS

PENNSYLVANIA HISTORICAL
AND MUSEUM COMMISSION

Kyle R. Weaver, Series Editor
Tracy Patterson, Designer

Published by
STACKPOLE BOOKS
5067 Ritter Road
Mechanicsburg, Pennsylvania 17055

Printed in the United States of America
10 9 8 7 6 5 4 3 2 1
FIRST EDITION

Maps by Caroline Stover

Photography
Craig A. Benner: cover, 3, 5, 6, 12, 20 (both), 22 (both), 35–47 (all)

Library of Congress Cataloging-in-Publication Data

Bradley, John.
    Ephrata Cloister : Pennsylvania trail of history guide / text by John Bradley.—1st ed.
      p. cm.—(Pennsylvania trail of history guides)
    Includes bibliographical references.
    ISBN 0-8117-2744-0
    1. Ephrata Cloister—Guidebooks. 2. Ephrata (Pa.)—Guidebooks. 3. Ephrata (Pa.)—Buildings, structures, etc.—Guidebooks. 4. Religious communities—Pennsylvania—Ephrata—History—18th century. 5. Pennsylvania—Religious life and customs—18th century. 6. Pennsylvania—History—Colonial period, ca. 1600-1775. I. Title. II. Series.

F159.E6 B73 2000
917.48'15—dc21
                                                     00-039493

Contents

Editor's Preface

S tackpole Books is pleased to present this volume of our Pennsylvania Trail of History Guides, an ongoing series of handbooks on the historic sites and museums administered by the Pennsylvania Historical and Museum Commission (PHMC).

The series was conceived and created by Stackpole Books with the cooperation of the PHMC's Division of Publications and Bureau of Historic Sites and Museums. The latter is headed by Donna Williams, and she and the bureau staff have lent their considerable expertise to the project. Diane Reed, Chief of Publications, has facilitated relations between the PHMC and Stackpole from the project's inception, organized the review process with the commission, and attended to numerous details related to the venture.

Michael Ripton, Director of the Ephrata Cloister, was the first person I approached, in early 1998, with the idea for a series of handbooks on Pennsylvania historic sites, and his guidance and encouragement led to the development of both the series and this particular book. Stephen Somers, former Curator of Collections at the Ephrata Cloister, patiently worked with me on several occasions, gathering transparencies of *Fraktur* and historic images from the site's vast collection. He also led me to the talented Craig A. Benner, who has captured the essence of the site in his photographs of historical reenactments and the interiors and exteriors of the buildings. Michael Showalter, Museum Educator at the Cloister, provided a thorough review of the manuscript.

John Bradley, the author of the text, is a Pennsylvania historian and teacher who has been involved with the Ephrata Cloister for most of his life. While in college he worked at the site as a groundskeeper and night watchman, and currently he is a volunteer tour guide and a member of the board of directors of the Ephrata Cloister Associates. With this ample experience, Bradley conveys the lifestyle and culture of the people who lived, worked, and worshiped in the buildings of the Ephrata Cloister; examines their place within William Penn's "holy experiment"; and provides insight on what remains at the site today.

Kyle R. Weaver, Editor
Stackpole Books

Introduction to the Site

The Ephrata Cloister, founded in 1732, housed a religious community built upon a shared set of beliefs first espoused by Conrad Beissel, the group's initial leader. The community, consisting of two celibate orders—a Brotherhood and a Sisterhood—and an order of married Householders, sought spiritual rather than material goals by practicing a lifestyle of discipline and self-deprivation. Ephrata became an important publishing center in the eighteenth century and was also known for the music and *Fraktur* that were created there.

Administered today by the Pennsylvania Historical and Museum Commission, the site includes nine original eighteenth-century buildings, three nineteenth-century structures, two graveyards, a spring, a visitor center, a museum store, and an amphitheater. Educational programs and cultural events are held on site frequently and are supported by the Ephrata Cloister Associates, a volunteer group founded in 1958.

Religion and Society in Colonial Pennsylvania

The Ephrata Cloister developed in a social setting that was unique for its time and place. In the eighteenth century, Pennsylvania hosted the most culturally diverse community to be found in any British North American colony. Men and women from many countries, speaking a variety of languages, and observing a multitude of religious faiths, lived side by side within the colony's borders. Pennsylvania's mixed society did not come about by accident; it was promoted by the colony's proprietor, William Penn. Soon after Old World immigrants began flooding into his province, Penn noted approvingly that "people of all sorts of nations and perswasions" were settling in Pennsylvania.

The son and namesake of a British admiral who was also a large landowner, William Penn was born in London in 1644. At age twenty-three, after study at Oxford and in France, Penn stunned his family by abandoning the Anglican faith (the Church of England) and joining the newly established Society of Friends, also known as Quakers. The Quakers were one of several dissenting faiths that came into existence in seventeenth-century England while the country was wracked by a bloody Civil War. The religious turmoil of the previous century, when King Henry VIII led the country out of the Roman Catholic Church rather than stay married to a wife he no longer wanted, carried on into the turbulent 1600s. Various nonconformist groups arose in England at that time, challenging church authorities and seeming to threaten the very stability of society.

England's religious traditions and disputes naturally played roles in the colonizing ventures that started in the reign of Henry's daughter, Elizabeth I, and continued under her successors of the House of Stuart. Virginia, established in 1607, and most of the other southern colonies were started by investors who represented the majority Church of England. Thus that church was established, or supported by taxes, in most of the colonies south of Pennsylvania. An exception was Maryland, founded by the

Religious Freedom, the hallmark of William Penn's colony, was a radical idea in the late seventeenth and early eighteenth centuries that allowed for the peaceful coexistence of many church groups in one small area and the development of new sects, such as the community at Ephrata.

Roman Catholic Lord Baltimore, who hoped to establish a place of refuge for his fellow Catholics.

In the northern colonies of New England, Puritan reformers dissatisfied with the structure, beliefs, and practices of the Church of England established their own form of Christian worship and excluded all others. Tiny Rhode Island was the region's outpost of religious freedom, admitting those who were stifled by the strictness of Puritan Massachusetts and Connecticut.

Because Quakers believed in social equality, refused military service, and rejected the Church of England, they were seen as dangerous heretics. They suffered persecution in England, and some of their leaders, such as William Penn, were imprisoned for their beliefs. But a fortunate circumstance put Penn in the good graces of King Charles II, enabling Penn to lead the Quakers to freedom in America.

Penn's father, the admiral, had helped Charles regain the throne after England's Civil War. Although many years had passed, Charles had never repaid Admiral Penn's £16,000 loan. Now with one act the king could honor the memory of his old friend who had died, clear up a debt, and rid England of a troublesome sect. In 1681 he granted Penn a charter to a colony that would be named Pennsylvania, meaning Penn's Woods.

Now the sole owner of one of the world's largest blocks of real estate, Penn made clear from the start that his new colony would be a laboratory for a "holy experiment": a test to see if men and women from different nations, speaking different languages, and believing in different faiths could live together in harmony. The experiment would also see whether such a community could pros-

per economically, providing a good life for its citizens and rewarding the proprietor, Penn. From the beginning, therefore, Penn hoped to establish in his colony "a blessed government and a virtuous, ingenious, and industrious society."

Pennsylvania's ethnic diversity actually preceded Penn's arrival. Along the Delaware River, in settlements nearly fifty years old, lived settlers from Finland and Sweden. These prior occupants were

8

soon submerged by the first wave of British settlers, many of them Quakers from England and Wales, who clustered in the southeastern corner of the new province in the three original counties of Bucks, Chester, and Philadelphia. Next, in 1683, one year after Penn's arrival, a group of immigrants established Germantown, a small community several miles from the colony's main settlement of Philadelphia. Historians continue to debate the exact origin of this

The Most Famous Image of William Penn, in treaty with the Lenape Indians under an elm, was rendered by many artists, inspired by Benjamin West's masterpiece of 1771. Quaker minister and folk artist Edward Hicks (1780–1849) painted this version, circa 1830, and executed the scene many more times during his life.

THE STATE MUSEUM OF PENNSYLVANIA
(GIFT OF MEYER P. AND VIVIAN POTAMKIN)

community: Were they Germans, as the name of their community would suggest, or were they ethnic Dutch, residents of the Netherlands?

The third major wave of immigrants to Colonial Pennsylvania also was of mixed origin. They were Protestants from Ulster, the north of Ireland, the descendants of settlers from Scotland who had been settled in Ireland by King James I a century earlier. Now, when economic hardships drove them to relocate to the New World, many of them chose Pennsylvania. Here there was abundant, cheap land and the freedom to practice their Presbyterian belief without interference from a hostile government. In Pennsylvania, these twice-uprooted settlers became known as the Scots-Irish to distinguish them from the native Roman Catholic Irish who were also present in Penn's colonies, although in smaller numbers.

Religious freedom in Pennsylvania owed its existence to William Penn, who welcomed adherents of all faiths. Clearly stated in the Great Law of 1682 was Penn's guarantee of freedom of conscience for all believers, as well as a statement granting protection from interference with any form of worship. Twenty years later, this promise was restated in another document, the Charter of Liberties, which reaffirmed the unqualified promise of religious freedom in Pennsylvania.

This concept, which Americans take for granted today, was a shocking departure from the practice of England and other European nations in the era of colonization. In most countries at that time, the official religion, which was supported by the monarch, had a jealously guarded monopoly on spiritual matters within each nation. Church officials worked closely with government leaders, each supporting the regulations of the other. This system, the only one familiar to most people, was accepted as the best way to ensure the well-being of the country. Seen in this light, Penn's decision to allow many religions to coexist in his province was a major challenge to a principle long accepted by church and state leaders.

Although Quakers predominated in Pennsylvania in the earliest years of the colony, it did not take long for them to lose their majority status as newcomers flocked to the province. From Britain came members of the Church of England, a faith later adopted by Penn's own sons, who inherited Pennsylvania upon his death. Many of the Welsh were Quakers, although others were Baptists, and most Scots-Irish were Presbyterians. Other early arrivals in Pennsylvania were persecuted Protestants from France called Huguenots. Small numbers of Catholics and Jews added to Pennsylvania's spiritual mix, but the greatest variety of faiths came with the arrival of thousands of newcomers from the Rhine River region of today's Germany.

About twenty-five years after the 1683 establishment of Germantown, the trickle of immigrants from the German-speaking regions of western Europe erupted into a flood. Germany would not be a unified nation for more than 150 years, and in the eighteenth century it was a confederation of hundreds of kingdoms, principalities, duchies, and other units, each governed by a ruling family. In most German territories, the religion of the king, duke, or prince was the official faith of the region. If the ruler died and was succeeded by a son who believed differently, the new faith was in power.

Most Germans, including most of those who left for America in the eighteenth century, were members of the two main Protestant churches, Lutheran and Reformed. It is estimated that 90 percent of the Colonial-era German immigrants were Lutheran or Reformed; they were called "church people" to distinguish them from the other 10 percent, the "sect people."

Christian sects, which may be thought of as splinter, or breakaway, groups, proliferated in the German lands in the late seventeenth and early eighteenth centuries, so it is not surprising that their members joined in the migration to the New World, Pennsylvania in particular, either to escape persecution or to better their economic status.

The first sect to arrive in Penn's colony were the Mennonites. Like the Scots-Irish, they were double migrants. Starting in the 1660s, they fled religious persecution in their native Switzerland to settle in the Palatinate of southwestern Germany. The Mennonites were later joined in Pennsylvania by their fellow Anabaptists, the more conservative Amish. Other German sects included the Moravians, primarily from southeastern Germany, a tiny group called Schwenkfelders, and another small group known as Brethren or Dunkers, who settled in the thriving village of Germantown. Taken together, about 100,000 German immigrants settled in Colonial Pennsylvania between 1683 and 1776.

Although most early-eighteenth-century Pennsylvanians probably identified with a particular religious tradition— Quaker, Mennonite, Anglican (Church of England), or Lutheran—historians indicate that many people were not par-

Pennsylvania in 1750. Three decades after the death of William Penn, religious freedom continued to thrive in Pennsylvania. The Ephrata community, located in Lancaster County, reached its highest peak with three hundred members.

ticularly observant members of their faiths. A shortage of pastors and the scattered nature of settlement in rural Pennsylvania contributed to this lack of religious enthusiasm.

With no compulsory church attendance laws, no tax-supported religious bodies, a multitude of faiths, and no favoritism or persecution of any of them, Pennsylvania truly demonstrated the success of the "holy experiment" envisioned by its founder. Economically, as well, the province was prospering. Farmers gathered bountiful harvests; towns and the one city, Philadelphia, grew; and trade flourished. In no other contemporary society anywhere in the world did such conditions prevail. The time, the place, and the conditions were right for the creation of the unique community at Ephrata.

History of the Ephrata Cloister

On the edge of Colonial Pennsylvania, where ethnic diversity and religious freedom flourished as in no other place in the eighteenth-century world, one community, Ephrata, stood out from all the others. Ephrata was the home of a religious group whose unique beliefs and practices were completely out of the American mainstream. Ephrata was a settlement where distinctive art, music, writing, and architecture flourished in Colonial days and remain today to be studied, admired, and analyzed. Ephrata was a monument to one man's spiritual journey, the power of his ideas, and the persuasiveness of his message.

Located in Lancaster County, about halfway between the major Colonial towns of Lancaster and Reading, Ephrata came into being in the first third of the eighteenth century. Not precisely a town or village, Ephrata was a community whose members shared a particular set of religious beliefs. It was religion that had called Ephrata into being, religion that furnished its rules and procedures, religion that shaped its outlook on society, and religion that dictated its quest for a unique relationship with God.

Some members of the Ephrata community rejected marriage on religious grounds, but marriage was not forbidden. Some members lived in large dormitories, having few personal possessions and spending their days in work, contemplation, and meditation. Others lived in ordinary homes, had farms of hundreds of acres, raised children, and lived in ways that were not so different from those of their Pennsylvania German neighbors.

At some point the nickname "Cloister" became applied to Ephrata, and that is the name by which the site has been known ever since. This is misleading, for the term *cloister* suggests a quiet, sheltered, withdrawn community, an oasis from the hustle and bustle of the larger, sinful world. To be sure, Ephrata had its moments of calm, humility, and peace, but at other times the community was wracked by dissension, tormented by challenges for leadership, and laden with energy when change, conflict, and disagreement filled the air. Today the name Ephrata Cloister refers to the historic site and is not applied to the living community of the past.

From its founding in 1732, Ephrata grew steadily, aided by the missionary zeal of its members and the religious revival known as the Great Awakening that was sweeping the colonies. The original handful of believers grew into a society of three hundred members at its high point in 1750. Decline, perhaps inevitable, set in as members grew older and new converts became increasingly difficult to find. With the death of the last of the single residents in the early 1800s, the remaining married members reestablished the community as a more conventional church and worshiped together for more than a century. Because they lived and held services in the original buildings, these masterpieces of eighteenth-century craftsmanship have endured until today.

But Ephrata is much more than buildings, fragile pieces of furniture, or religious books written in the obscure German vocabulary of its residents. Ephrata is a monument to the energy, vision, and thought of its guiding light, a refugee from Germany who found in Pennsylvania the fertile soil in which to plant his unique religious concepts and watch them grow into a society unlike any other in the world. This refugee's name was Conrad Beissel, and from his mind and heart came the Ephrata community.

EPHRATA'S FOUNDER

Conrad Beissel was born in 1691 in the village of Eberbach in the Palatinate region of southwestern Germany. At this time, the Palatinate was slowly recovering from the devastation it had suffered during a series of European wars that used the area as a battleground because of its central location among the fighting nations. Citizens displaced by warfare, combined with newcomers moving in from surrounding areas, gave the Palatinate a diversified, but economically impoverished, population.

Young Conrad never knew his father, who had died shortly before the boy's birth. Then, when he was only eight, his mother died. Family members took in

the orphan and soon afterward apprenticed him to a baker in Eberbach. This was Beissel's first step on the long journey toward certification as a master baker and membership in the bakers' guild. Most crafts or trades were governed by guilds, whose members set standards for their products, established prices, and oversaw the training of new members. Apprenticeship, which might last five, seven, or more years, was the first step. An apprentice would learn the skills needed for baking, but before he could become a full-fledged member of the bakers' guild, he would have to spend several years as a journeyman. The journeyman traveled from town to town, finding work with various master bakers, to polish the skills and demonstrate his mastery of the intricacies of the bread-making craft.

It was during Beissel's years as a journeyman, as he traveled among the towns and cities of the Palatinate, that he came into contact with numerous groups of religious dissenters, who, much like the Quakers in England, were critical of the established churches and offered their own views on spirituality. Beissel grew up in the German Reformed Church, but as he read the works of independent religious thinkers and theologians, he appears to have been impressed by their arguments. One particular author whose works had a major impact on Beissel and later on the Ephrata community was Jakob Boehme. Boehme introduced Beissel to Mysticism, the concept that a believer should seek a personal, close, intense relationship with God. For a mystic, no pastor or other intermediary was necessary; the believer could communicate directly with God, listen and be understood by Him, and thus achieve a peace and comfort not available in any other way.

Presumed to Be Conrad Beissel. *This silhouette of a young man has been identified for many years as an "alleged" portrait of Conrad Beissel.* EPHRATA CLOISTER COLLECTION

Another religious development that influenced Beissel was Pietism, a movement that started in German churches in the late seventeenth century. For Pietists, religious formality as seen in liturgies, published statements of belief, or creeds was not nearly so important as the personal and emotional aspects of religion that the individual believer experienced. In some towns, Pietist groups gathered for discussion, mutual support, and the sharing of religious feelings. Most Pietists did not intend to separate from their churches but merely to introduce these new concepts into their spiritual lives. However, one extreme group called the Radical Pietists found no room for their ideas in the existing churches. They were true separatists who wanted to break free from all established religious organizations.

As Beissel became absorbed in religious thought, especially the more

CHRONOLOGY

1691	Conrad Beissel is born in Eberbach, Germany
1720	Beissel arrives in Philadelphia
1724	Beissel becomes leader of the Conestoga Brethren congregation
1732	Beissel leaves the Conestoga Brethren to live as a religious "solitary"
1735	The Ephrata community is organized and builds *Kedar*, the first large building
1740–55	High point of the Ephrata community
1768	Conrad Beissel dies at age seventy-seven
1777–78	Ephrata used as hospital for wounded Continental soldiers
1796	Peter Miller, Beissel's successor, dies at age eighty-six
1813	Last two celibate sisters die
1814	Householders form the German Religious Society of Seventh-Day Baptists
1934	German Seventh-Day Baptist congregation is dissolved
1941	Pennsylvania Historical and Museum Commission acquires the Ephrata Cloister
1958	Ephrata Cloister Associates founded

extreme ideas of the Mystics and of the Radical Pietists, his participation in dissenting groups came to the attention of the authorities. Because he refused to attend or support the established church, Beissel was expelled from the Palatinate in 1718.

The twenty-nine-year-old baker now joined a flood of emigrants, estimated at nearly 1 million, who left the Palatinate in the early eighteenth century. Most of these nomads went to Eastern Europe: to Hungary, Russia, or the Ukraine. About one-sixth turned westward and aimed for Britain's American colonies. A few were religious refugees like Beissel, although the vast majority were those suffering from economic hardship. Where would he go? Pennsylvania beckoned.

Beissel thus joined the steadily increasing stream of immigrants from the German states, and the Palatinate in particular, into William Penn's colony. Penn had first become acquainted with Germany in the 1670s, when he made three mission trips up the Rhine River, playing a part in converting some Germans to the Quaker faith. Always hoping to make Pennsylvania economically stable, Penn knew of the Germans' skill at agriculture and realized that these hardy farmers would help his province's material growth.

Beissel arrived in Philadelphia, a city of ten thousand residents, in 1720. He came two years after the death of William Penn and three years before a penniless runaway from Boston named Benjamin Franklin came to town. Beissel hoped to connect with a small band of German Radical Pietists who had established a community near Philadelphia in 1694. He expected to find them near the Wissahickon Creek, waiting for Christ's Second Coming, which they believed would happen at any moment. The members of this community, known as the Society of the Woman in the Wilderness, were unmarried men who endured lives of self-denial and devoted all of their attention to achieving the mystic union with God that Beissel was also searching for. To Beissel's dismay, he learned that the group, led by the religious enthusiast Johannes Kelpius, had disbanded several years before his arrival.

Unable to join the Kelpius community, Beissel decided to settle in Pennsylvania's oldest and largest German community, Germantown. Here he found work with a weaver named Peter Becker. This was a fateful move on Beissel's part, for Becker not only employed and housed the former baker, but also introduced Beissel to another small religious community, the German Baptists, or Brethren. Also called Dunkers for their practice of baptizing adults by full immersion, the Brethren were a group that, like Beissel, had been influenced by the Mystics and Pietists of the Old World. They had arrived in Pennsylvania one year before Beissel, but had not yet begun to function as a congregation. Now Peter Becker and his new assistant, Conrad Beissel, were about to change that.

As Becker began to organize the Brethren of Germantown and those living in other communities near Philadelphia, he also developed an interest in establishing a congregation in the Conestoga region, the area that would later become known as Lancaster County. Traveling to the area in 1724, Becker and Beissel found a number of people receptive to their message, and a little congregation was organized, with Conrad Beissel chosen to serve as the pastor.

During Beissel's time as pastor of the Conestoga Brethren, he began to preach and write about the ideas he had been assembling over the past few years during his travels in Germany and his brief

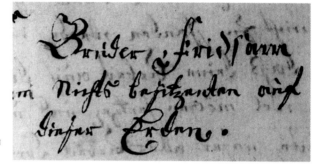

Beissel's Signature.
Members of the Ephrata
community took new names,
further disconnecting them-
selves from their past lives.
Beissel was known at
Ephrata as Brother Fried-
sam, as this signature indi-
cates. EPHRATA CLOISTER COLLECTION

time in America. From the influence of the Mystics, writers like Boehme, the Radical Pietists, and other religious commentators, Beissel began to expound his thoughts about Christian belief and practice. He taught that the goal of the Christian was the individual soul's union with God. To achieve this union, all other concerns had to be denied, including economic success, material possessions, and any degree of comfort, ease, or rest. In fact, wrote Beissel, suffering was paramount; it was the only way to achieve the desired union with God.

Next, Beissel turned his attention to the key units of human relationships, marriage and the family. Marriage was not for the true Christian, Beissel wrote. Only celibacy would free the believer from earthly concerns and enable him to focus all of his attention on following his goal: the path toward union with God. In fact, the believer's relationship with God would be a kind of marriage. From Jakob Boehme he took the concept that God was a being of both genders, male and female. God's female aspect, "Heavenly Sophia," personified "Pure, Godly, and Heavenly Wisdom," wrote Beissel. He thought that male celibates should pursue a "spiritual marriage" with Sophia, just as female believers should consider themselves married to Jesus Christ, God's male half.

To his concepts of union with God, suffering, and celibacy, Beissel added a

fourth tenet. Convinced that Christians who worshiped on Sunday had chosen the wrong Sabbath, Beissel began to advocate the traditional Jewish day of rest, from sundown on Friday to sundown on Saturday. This belief is known as Sabbatarianism, or the observance of the Seventh-Day Sabbath.

Finally, hearkening back to the teachings of his Pietist mentors, Beissel began to stress the need for separation from the larger world. This did not signify isolation or a complete shutting off of all contact from society. Beissel conceived of separation as a withdrawing of like-minded believers into a special association. Here they could share their spiritual experiences and search for the desired union with God.

As Beissel's mind took him farther and farther away from conventional Brethren belief and more deeply into a theology of his own construction, he became dissatisfied with his status in life. In 1732 he left the congregation. Now he was free to follow his own spiritual path and seek his personal union with God.

Several miles away was a site on the gentle Cocalico Creek, where Beissel found room in a settler's crude hut. On the banks of the meandering Cocalico—*Koch-Halekung* or "Den of Serpents," in the language of the Native Americans—Beissel could now contemplate a life free from all responsibility except the cultivation of his own spiritual development. He would live as a hermit, in his own space, and travel the mystic route toward connection with God at his own pace. He could begin to train his body and his soul to anticipate paradise. But Conrad Beissel's days as a lone seeker of the truth would not be many.

THE EMERGENCE OF EPHRATA

Some of Beissel's former followers in the Conestoga Brethren congregation had believed his teachings on the way to get close to God, and they came to Beissel's cabin on the Cocalico to hear his message. Gradually a small fellowship began to take shape, a loose-knit collection of believers who personified the Pietist ideal of the gathered community that emphasized experience and emotion rather than formal church structure.

In 1735 Beissel made a momentous decision: To restructure his informal congregation, he directed the scattered believers—hermits like himself, or "solitaries" as they called themselves—to transform their community of fellowship into a physical reality. Ephrata, a Biblical name denoting suffering, was chosen as the name for the small settlement. "So then Ephrata is now built up out of this soil of suffering," recorded the *Ephrata Chronicle*, the society's official history, of the time when all of the dispersed solitaries came together by the Cocalico.

In that same year, Beissel instructed his followers to build a large dormitory. In short order, the large structure named *Kedar* was constructed. It housed the celibate men and women and contained prayer rooms, work space, and eating facilities. Beissel's motives for building *Kedar* are unclear. Did he think the structure would unite the community in its attempt to "oppose the world?" Or did he see this as a means to solidify his control over his followers?

As Ephrata grew, it developed into a community consisting of three separate religious orders closely interlinked with one another. The celibate men formed an organization known as the Brotherhood, while unmarried women made up the Sisterhood. For these people, nothing would interfere with their quest for union with God. That quest became all-consuming, leading the believers to devote all of their waking hours to spiritual matters. Life at Ephrata became a testing ground for the celibates, as they struggled to learn the discipline and endure the suffering that would lead to eternal happiness.

Although one of Conrad Beissel's primary teachings was the superiority of celibacy over marriage, among his earliest followers were married persons who shared all of his views except this key point. These members, known as Householders, were Ephrata's third order. They did not reside directly at the settlement itself, but rather lived on their own lands in the surrounding countryside. The Householders were always a large numerical presence at Ephrata, and they were also influential in shaping policy and direction for the community as well. Their presence illustrates a key concept that gave Ephrata part of its identity: In this community, hard-and-fast rules were the exception rather than the norm. Beissel's teachings were often presented as "it is better not to marry," not a blanket condemnation of the practice. This is in accord with the Pietist insistence on the primacy of the individual's experience, not the establishment of inflexible, traditional laws, rules, or precepts.

Membership in the new society grew in response to its active missionary work. Beissel and other members traveled to German-speaking communities in Pennsylvania and New Jersey in search of converts. Beissel's published

Bethania, *the Brothers' House.* *The dormitory for the celibate Brotherhood was built in 1746. It was torn down in the early twentieth century because of deterioration.*

writings circulated in those communities, taking his persuasive message to the receptive. He continued to maintain close relationships with the Brethren community, not only at Conestoga, his former congregation, but also with other groups in Pennsylvania, including Germantown, the sect's American home. Although individuals from many religious backgrounds and from several nationalities joined the Ephrata society over the years, former members of the Brethren faith were always among the most numerous.

As the Great Awakening, a period of revived interest in religion, swept America, Beissel took advantage of the fervor to press his drive for attracting new members. The year 1735 saw him win two prominent converts from the Tulpehocken region north of Ephrata, in what is now Berks County. Here Beissel attracted a prominent landowner,

farmer, and merchant named Conrad Weiser, Pennsylvania's "ambassador" to the Iroquois Indians. He also persuaded Weiser's neighbor, Peter Miller, an ordained German Reformed pastor, theologian, and university graduate, to move to Ephrata. Miller remained at Ephrata for the rest of his life; Weiser, however, broke away in 1743.

Entire families joined the community in response to Beissel's evangelizing. Usually these families would become part of the Householder group, but in some instances, husband and wife would separate, each going into the respective celibate order. On occasion, only one member of a couple would come to Ephrata. Maria Sauer, whose husband, Christopher, was Pennsylvania's first German-language printer, was one of these converts. Indian agent Weiser similarly left a wife at home in the Tulpehocken. Such behavior raised eyebrows and led

19

some people to speculate about the goings-on at the unusual new community along the Cocalico Creek.

EPHRATA'S ARCHITECTURE: PHYSICAL AND SYMBOLIC

The success of Beissel's evangelizing led to an increasing membership roll at the community and the need for more buildings. Over the eleven years following the construction of *Kedar* in 1735, almost one new dormitory, chapel, or other structure was put up at Ephrata every year. The settlement grew out from its center into a triangular shape; for a mystic like Beissel, the triangle was a symbol of perfection. One set of buildings clustered near the top of a rise called Mount Zion, which overlooked the Cocalico; others rose east and west of *Kedar*, equidistant from the community's center.

Male members of the community, Householders and Brothers, built all of its structures over the years, using the abundant wood and stone from the area. Their models were the buildings they remembered from the Palatinate and neighboring regions of Germany and Switzerland. Unlike most Colonial American architecture, which followed British examples, the Germanic structures at Ephrata had several distinctive features, including steeply pitched roofs punctuated by multiple dormer windows. Large central chimneys mark the locations of clay-lined fireplaces used for

Ephrata's Architecture. A view of Saron *from above reveals the characteristic steep roof, dormer windows, and A-shaped chimneys of the Germanic buildings at Ephrata. The window placement on the* Saal *shows that symmetry was not as much a concern for the architects at Ephrata as it was for those in the rest of Colonial America.*

heating the massive structures and for cooking the community's meals. Ephrata buildings usually are not symmetrical, their windows are small, and their doors are both narrow and low. The steep roofs were covered with oak shingles (replaced in recent years with cedar), doubly overlapped and nailed to protect them from the harsh winds of winter.

The builders used two different methods to construct Ephrata's community buildings. In the half-timbered, or *Fachwerk*, style, the exterior walls are made of frames built of heavy timbers, with stone and mud packed into the open spaces. This method was commonly used in northern Europe and was certainly familiar to the carpenter crews. The exteriors of Ephrata's *Fachwerk* buildings are covered with clapboard, and the inside walls are plastered and whitewashed.

Most German settlers found that half-timbered buildings were not appropriate for Pennsylvania's climate, so they switched to log structures. The same is true at Ephrata, where about half of the later surviving historic buildings are made of huge logs notched at the corners, packed with mud mortar, and then clapboarded and plastered. Materials that the community was not able to provide for itself included window glass, raw iron for the hinges, other hardware, and specialized tools. These had to be obtained from merchants in Philadelphia or in the growing town of Lancaster, only thirteen miles to the south. Ephrata was not self-sufficient, nor did it attempt to completely isolate itself from "the world."

RELIGIOUS PRACTICES

At Ephrata, a primary focus of religious activity was the individual believer's progress toward the goal of uniting with God. For the celibates, every human activity was experienced in terms of its

THE *HEBRON* EXPERIMENT

The Sisters' House was originally built as part of one of the most interesting episodes at Ephrata, an adventure known as the *Hebron* Experiment. This plan encouraged married couples of the Householder congregation to separate, leave their individual homes, and move into this new building called *Hebron* (many Ephrata buildings had biblical names). As originally constructed in 1743, the building had dividing walls separating each of the three floors in half, with the men living on one side of the partitions and the women on the other. The Householders' children were left with friends or family members during this experiment, which lasted only about eighteen months. At that point, in 1745, the dividing partitions were torn down, the couples reunited, and they resumed family life in their own homes. The building was given to the Sisters, who had been living in another dormitory, and was renamed *Saron*.

usefulness in bringing the individual closer to that goal. But Ephrata also provided group religious experiences that helped bind the community together and enhance each participant's progress along the mystic pilgrimage.

The Ephrata Sabbath was Saturday, in accordance with Beissel's teaching. On that day, the community—celibates and Householders—would gather in one of the meetinghouses, women and men sitting separately. Beissel usually presided over the service, which was simple and unstructured, in keeping with the Pietist emphasis on the believer's inner experience. Scripture readings, generally from the Old Testament or from the book of Revelation, were an important element. The choir sang *a cappella* chorales and anthems, and Beissel gave a sermon. One observer reported that Beissel

The love feast was the most important ritual celebrated at Ephrata. It consisted of three parts: foot washing, a fellowship meal, and holy communion. The Brethren Church, source of many members of the Ephrata community, held love feasts in imitation of the earliest Christians. This was evidently the inspiration for Ephrata's ritual.

To begin the ceremony, participants washed and dried each other's feet. This humbling act can symbolize a cleansing from sin, although at Ephrata foot washing was also an indication of hospitality. Next they shared a meal that was more filling than the usual community fare. With the usual ban on meat relaxed for the occasion, the congregation enjoyed mutton that evening. Finally, the bread and wine of communion were served. Conrad Beissel always insisted on leading this segment of the ritual.

The community held love feasts frequently, but not according to a fixed schedule. Sometimes the ceremonies, which were always held in the evening, lasted five or six hours. In his precommunion sermons Beissel blasted his followers for their sins, no doubt at length.

Love feasts were held on a variety of occasions and could involve the entire congregation or just selected individuals. At times, the Brothers or the Sisters held love feasts for their group only. A particular Householder family could have a ceremony for a small number of guests. Everyone was included in the celebration as a new building was consecrated. A love feast also might be held in honor of a member who had died. Some residents of Ephrata left money in their wills to pay the costs of memorial love feasts for themselves.

preached without notes, grimacing one moment, closing his eyes the next, and waving his arms about as he spoke.

A special moment of the service was the time set aside for public testimonials from members of the group. Anyone could make a comment, express a feeling, or describe an experience that was particularly significant. Prayer was silent. No doubt the spontaneous character of worship at Ephrata appealed to the individuals who found the conventional churches' highly patterned services unfulfilling.

After the service, which normally lasted one and a half hours, the community members walked back to their dwellings to spend the rest of the day alone in their small sleeping rooms. Here they could study, pray, or meditate while observing the injunction against laboring on the Sabbath.

The Sisterhood and Brotherhood also held worship services every evening at midnight. Awakening from sleep, they walked to their separate chapels for the two-hour sessions, which were similar in format to the Sabbath services. The late hour was chosen because Christ's Second Coming was expected to be at midnight.

The Ephrata love feast was an activity that combined spiritual friendship with elements of worship. A meal of fellowship, it was based on the practices of the earliest Christians and was viewed as a way to prepare for Christ's Second Coming. A love feast might involve the entire community or be shared by a smaller group.

DISCIPLINE THROUGH LABOR

Work occupied a central place at Ephrata, but for very different reasons than in the outside world. Unlike in the capitalist, free-enterprise system slowly developing in the American colonies, Ephrata displayed little interest in amassing wealth for its own sake. The community also rejected material progress, economic competition, or the status other Americans accorded to land, possessions, or influence. Instead, work at Ephrata took place in reference to the community's chief goal: preparation of the individual member for a mystic union with God, brought about by suffering. Suffering was all important, taught Beissel. To endure suffering and to keep focused on the goal, one must learn discipline. And what better way to

Work at Ephrata *was a form of discipline intended to bring members closer to God.* EPHRATA CLOISTER COLLECTION

learn discipline than through work—not work for wages, preference, or advancement, but work as a means of glorifying God through the labor and skill of one's body.

The Ephrata workday was as rigidly structured as the Sabbath was spontaneous. Awake at 5:00 A.M., the Brothers and Sisters worked for nine hours, with four one-hour periods reserved for prayer and meditation. Add on two hours for formal study in the early evening, two hours for the midnight worship, and one hour for eating, and all that is left for sleep is six hours.

In keeping with eighteenth-century norms, men and women did very different kinds of work at Ephrata. Many of the Brothers, like most of their Pennsylvania German neighbors, were farmers. They grew grains and flax, whose stringy fibers can be spun into linen. They cleared areas of trees and tended orchards. They also raised animals. Some Brothers worked in the community's water-powered mills that sat along the Cocalico. Here they sawed boards, ground wheat and rye into flour, made paper, and pressed flaxseed into linseed oil. Others operated a tannery where animal skins were processed into leather. Bakers were important, too, for bread was one of the basic foodstuffs in the community. Printers turned out single handbills called broadsides, works on theology, and hymnals for the community and a variety of other products for paying customers. Other Brothers were shoemakers, tailors, and weavers. The Brothers did their own cooking, cleaning, and laundry.

Rules of the Sisterhood prohibited the members from joking, gossiping, and laughing while they were at work, "so that our life be modest, quiet, tranquil, and retired." Sisters planted and tended the gardens, picking the vegetables, roots, and herbs that were important parts of the community's diet. Some spun wool and flax yarn for the Brothers to weave. Then seamstresses sewed clothing for the community, while other Sisters made candles or wove baskets of rye straw.

DIET AND DRESS

Because of Beissel's stress on suffering, it is not surprising that this concept, when applied at Ephrata, led to a denial of many comforts, pleasures, or even necessities of life. The large buildings were heated only by open fireplaces and crude, five-plate iron stoves; no heat sources were available in the members' sleeping chambers, or *Kammer*. And ironically, given Ephrata's location in a rich agricultural area, the members chose to limit their intake of food.

The celibate groups at Ephrata ate just one cooked meal daily, which was served at 6:00 P.M. They ate bread, vegetable greens, cabbage, beets, and cheese curds. The orchard supplied fruit, which the Brothers and Sisters usually ate dried or cooked. One visitor was served pumpkin mush and boiled barley. He was not impressed. Beissel prohibited some foods, such as beans, because they "awaken impure desires." He urged his followers not to eat meat or fatty foods. Ephrata's beverage of choice was water.

Some members of the community fasted periodically, because they thought that would help them to see God's presence. Many ate small quantities of food and restricted themselves to the approved diet, believing that this means of self-denial would bring them closer to God. It is likely that the Householders did not eat the meager Ephrata diet. Evidence suggests that they and their chil-

dren consumed a more standard amount and variety of food.

The sparse diet of Ephrata was probably no worse than the one consumed by peasants back in the Palatinate. Because of its high cost, the poor there rarely ate meat. But compared with other Pennsylvanians, the celibates at Ephrata were definitely worse off in terms of nutrition. Contemporary descriptions of community members as gaunt and thin are probably accurate.

Most commentators were intrigued by the appearance of Ephrata's Brothers and Sisters, for their clothing was most unconventional. To emphasize the community's spiritual focus, its members wore robed garments like those of monastic societies in Europe. Men and women alike wore a long, sacklike garment that covered the body from the shoulders to the feet. Over this they wore a scapular, a long piece of cloth similar to an apron. Brothers wore pointed cloth hoods that covered most of the head and face but not their long beards. The Sisters' hoods were rounded. Cloth belts went around their waists.

These garments were made of linen in the summer and wool in the winter, and were off-white in color. Wool stockings and crude leather shoes were permitted, but most people went barefoot. The shapeless robes hid the body, muffling physical attractiveness and blotting out distinctions between men and women and between individual members of the society.

THE ARTS
At Ephrata, the spiritual quest toward union with God was evident in all aspects of life. This extended to the community's creative endeavors in the areas of music and hand-drawn illustration. Music played an enormous part in the life of the Ephrata community, for it had a central role in worship and offered directions for the difficult journey toward the presence of God.

Some of America's earliest original music was composed at Ephrata by more than fifty individuals. The prolific Beissel produced almost half of the one thousand hymns written by the community.

Fraktur. *The Sisters and Brothers created the ornate illuminations for manuscripts, wall charts, and bookplates. The motifs—roses, lilies, hearts, turtledoves—relate to biblical passages.* EPHRATA CLOISTER COLLECTION (ABOVE AND OPPOSITE)

Apparently having some natural talent for music, he learned composition slowly, developing harmonization charts that enabled him to create songs with four, six, or seven parts. Brothers and Sisters formed the Ephrata choirs, often with women singing the top three parts, and men the bass alone.

The Ephrata choirs practiced diligently, sometimes for three or four hours at a time, in an attempt to achieve the unique sound demanded by Beissel. He became choirmaster several years after the community's beginning. Eighteenth-century visitors provide intriguing details about the sound of Ephrata

THE CHRISTIAN ABC BOOK

Perhaps the best-known example of Ephrata *Fraktur* is the *Christian ABC Book,* completed in 1750. "The Christian A B C is Suffering, Patience, and Hope, Who Has Attained These Has Reached His Goal," the title page declares. This large manuscript begins with two complete alphabets, one letter per page. One alphabet has elaborate borders, while the second does not. Next, a third complete alphabet having four letters to a page, then a variety of

letters and numerals. Although both Sisters and Brothers produced *Fraktur,* the *ABC Book* appears to have been created by the women. It was once thought to have been a book of style for the elaborate wall charts, but its unwieldy size makes such use unlikely. Human figures, crudely drawn, appear in some of the letters. The capital *B,* for example, includes an image of John the Apostle, author of a gospel and the book of Revelation.

music. One such visitor, Anglican minister Jacob Duché of Philadelphia, wrote of the "sweet, shrill, and small voices" of the choir. Others described music that seemed to hover overhead rather than come directly from the mouths of the singers; it seemed light, airy, and otherworldly. Their heads bent forward, lips barely moving, the choir members sounded to some listeners like gentle turtledoves.

Nothing produced at Ephrata surpasses the beauty of the delicate handdrawn illustrations known as *Fraktur,* a shortened form of *Frakturschriften.* Examples of this folk art form include bookplates, illustrated music manuscripts, and large wall charts displaying religious poetry. Ephrata's *Fraktur* was the first produced in America. All of the Pennsylvania German groups created *Fraktur,* in such forms as marriage licenses, birth and baptismal certificates, and house blessings.

Drawing on paper produced at the community's mill, Ephrata's *Fraktur* artists spent countless hours perfecting their technique and then many more hours carefully inking their designs. They used pale red, green, and blue tones to highlight the delicate roses and lilies that ornament the personal music books, adding other figures such as sunflowers, pomegranates, and doves. Because all of this flora and fauna had symbolic meaning for Ephrata, the *Fraktur* was always much more than mere decoration. In addition, the discipline required to complete the work was seen as part of the suffering that would help the artist arrive in Paradise.

Public *Fraktur* at Ephrata took the form of large charts, some as big as 4 feet square, which hung on the walls in prominent locations throughout the community. These charts presented biblical sayings or original devotional verses, written in a Gothic German script. They illustrate well the literal meaning of *Frakturschriften*—"broken writing"—because the letters seem to have been composed of individual segments that were split apart and then reassembled.

PRINTING

Beissel recognized the power of the printed word early in his ministry. During the decades of the 1720s and 1730s, he arranged to have several of his writings published in Philadelphia by Benjamin Franklin and others. As the community expanded, however, the congregation purchased its own printing press, lead type, and other equipment from Germany and began to produce its own imprints. The Brothers' paper mill supplied sheets of fine-quality linen rag paper, while Ephrata made its own ink by adding lampblack to boiling linseed oil. Leather for book covers came from the tannery.

The press of the Brotherhood turned out more than 125 publications in its fifty years in operation. These included collections of essays, books on theology, a German edition of Bunyan's *Pilgrim's Progress*, and histories. A new Ephrata hymnal, *The Turtledove*, published in

THE MARTYRS' MIRROR

EPHRATA CLOISTER COLLECTION

One of the better-known products of the Brotherhood's press was an ambitious project undertaken in conjunction with the Mennonite community of southeastern Pennsylvania. Descendants of the Anabaptists, early Protestant reformers in the Netherlands and in Switzerland, the Mennonites were acutely conscious of their history, especially of the lives of people who had suffered or died for their beliefs. In 1660 Thieleman Jansz van Braght compiled a history of the persecutions of Christian martyrs from the early days of Christianity through the horrific Counter-Reformation of the sixteenth and seventeenth centuries. Titled *The Martyrs' Mirror*, the book was originally published in the Netherlands. Pennsylvania's Mennonites, primarily of Swiss-German extraction, wanted a German language edition of van Braght's work. In 1747 they struck a deal with the Cloister press to produce thirteen hundred copies of this massive fifteen-hundred-page work.

The text was translated into German by Peter Miller, the former Reformed pastor, who was skillful in language. Miller also worked with the crew of Brothers who printed the pages by hand, weathering paper shortages and other difficulties until the massive book was completed in 1749. It told of the beheadings, mutilations, and other atrocities visited upon the martyrs, including the account of the death of Hans Landis in 1614. Landis, an Anabaptist pastor from Zurich, Switzerland, had numerous family members in the Pennsylvania Mennonite community.

29

1747, was one of the first collections of original music composed in America. Single sheets known as "broadsides," small booklets, and legal forms such as land deeds were also issued. For the Mennonites of Pennsylvania, the Brothers produced a German edition of *The Martyrs' Mirror*, the largest book printed in America during the Colonial period.

A SCHISM IN THE COMMUNITY

The most significant split within the Ephrata community started in the settlement's second decade, with a move by some of the male celibates to emphasize the commercial, economic aspects of the society. At this time, both the Brotherhood and Sisterhood were led by Beissel appointees called prior and prioress, and each group had considerable autonomy within the larger sphere of the Ephrata community. Israel Eckerlin, prior of the Brotherhood, supported by his biological brothers Samuel and Emanuel, wanted to stress the financial possibilities of the community's mills. This was a direction that Beissel and his supporters in the community feared would weaken the spiritual emphasis that had been the reason for the community's founding. Each side in the dispute had its advocates, and for a while it looked as if the Eckerlin faction would triumph. But finally Beissel reasserted his authority and ordered the expulsion of the Eckerlin faction.

This schism weakened but did not destroy Ephrata, which was still enjoying the decade of its highest significance. The Eckerlins journeyed southwest, into the Shenandoah Valley, where they attempted to create a second Ephrata in the wilderness. Israel and Gabriel were captured by the French during the French and Indian War and taken as prisoners to Canada. Samuel and other members of the breakaway faction returned to Ephrata in 1764, moving into a house on Mount Zion and claiming ownership of the community's land based on old deeds executed years before. Now the community was faced with the odd situation of housing two rival groups living within sight of each other. We can only wonder what their interactions, if any, were on a day-to-day basis. Further research and future archaeological digs on the site could provide clues on how this conflict was resolved.

DECLINE AND CHANGE

From 1750, when the Ephrata community—Sisters, Brothers, and Householders, totaled about three hundred persons—the society slowly began to decline. The original members, Beissel and his first followers, were getting older, and their ability to evangelize among new immigrants was waning.

One positive accomplishment of Ephrata's second two decades was the establishment of several offshoot communities farther west in Pennsylvania. German Seventh-Day Baptist congregations with roots at Ephrata still exist at Snow Hill, near Waynesboro in Franklin County, and Salemville, Bedford County. Members of these churches come to Ephrata annually to worship and hold love feasts in the place where their faith had its origin.

The biggest blow to Ephrata's continuation as a unique religious community came in 1768 with the death of Conrad Beissel at age seventy-seven. Ephrata was largely the product of his creative mind, his compelling personality, and his persistence in the conduct of his spiritual quest. The mourners who gathered at his graveside knew that they were seeing the end of an era.

Peter Miller, the man who had served as Beissel's second in command for many years, now assumed the

Beissel's Grave. *Ephrata's founder and leader is buried in God's Acre, a graveyard at Ephrata. The stone of his successor, Peter Miller, stands to the left.*

EPHRATA CLOISTER COLLECTION

leader's post at Ephrata. Scholarly, gentle, given more to compromise than to confrontation, Miller assumed control with resignation, knowing that the Ephrata way of life would not long continue. Although he knew that the thinking of the larger American society was changing and that the Ephrata way of life no longer had the appeal it once had, Miller continued to insist on staying apart from "the world." "Remember, the most beaten path is wrong," he counseled. Instead of mounting a publicity or recruitment drive, Miller was

Peter Miller. *The erudite successor to Beissel is believed to be Agrippa, the coauthor of the Ephrata history* Chronicon Ephratense.

EPHRATA CLOISTER COLLECTION

content to continue in his life of quiet contemplation, seeing the approach of the inevitable end but feeling unable to do anything to prevent it.

The Ephrata society had been largely apolitical throughout its existence, leaving such mundane concerns as governance, taxation, and public policy to the people of the outside world. During the French and Indian War (1756–63), the community was far enough from the frontier to avoid any of the skirmishing that terrorized more westerly sections of Pennsylvania. In the next two decades, the community was oblivious to the tax protests and philosophical arguments that grabbed so much attention in Colonial America. Ephrata had no use for questions about Parliamentary supremacy or taxation without representation.

Clinging to their pacifist roots, the remaining Brothers at Ephrata did not serve in the armed struggle that became the American Revolution in 1775, although it is possible that several Householders took up arms in support of the patriot cause. Their community escaped the line of fire, but the British invasion of Pennsylvania and march on Philadelphia in the autumn of 1777 did have repercussions for Ephrata.

On September 11, 1777, a large British army under the leadership of

Military Hospital. Though pacifists, the community operated a hospital for wounded soldiers during the Revolutionary War.
EPHRATA CLOISTER COLLECTION

Gen. Sir William Howe, accompanied by several regiments of mercenaries from the German state of Hesse, encountered George Washington's Continental Army at the Brandywine River in Chester County, about 40 miles east of Ephrata. In savage fighting, both sides experienced heavy losses in what is known as the single bloodiest day of the war. The victorious British pushed through Washington's defenses, continuing on their march to America's capital at Philadelphia, then proceeding to occupy that city throughout the following winter.

Because the American army had practically no provisions for the care of wounded soldiers, these unfortunates were sheltered in temporary quarters throughout southeastern Pennsylvania. In December of that year, a military hospital was established at Ephrata, in one of the older buildings on Mount Zion. With the era's primitive knowledge of sanitation, a hospitalized soldier was much more likely to die than was one serving in combat. Today a marble obelisk marks the common grave of the Colonial soldiers who died at Ephrata, in a strange interlude in the life of a withdrawn community that wanted nothing more than to separate from the larger, dangerous world beyond the settlement's limits.

Following the Americans' victory at Yorktown and the winning of independence in 1783, Ephrata must have seemed more and more like a quaint, irrelevant, out-of-the-way spot that time was forgetting. America was transfixed, with dreams of republicanism, democracy, and economic independence filling the air. Now Peter Miller's prophecy of Ephrata's end seemed even more imminent, and this end was greatly hastened by Miller's own death in 1796. Less than twenty years later, in 1813, the last of the celibates—two unmarried Sisters—also died. Ephrata, the camp of the solitary, the vale of suffering, would have to make a great transformation or cease existing.

But there were members of the Householder congregation who had the courage to carry on the message of Conrad Beissel and the first solitaries. In 1814 the German Religious Society of Seventh-Day Baptists was incorporated, and this congregation continued to occupy the old buildings, work the fields, and worship in the Sisters' meetinghouse. It is only because of the married congregation's determination to preserve the best of the old traditions that any remnant of Ephrata exists today. As the years went by, some assets of the old community were sold off to neighbors, including the printing press, several of the mills, and some of the outlying acreage.

Several times in the nineteenth and twentieth centuries, the congregation was beset by internal disputes. After the last of these, in 1929, the Pennsylvania Department of Justice revoked the congregation's charter. In 1934, the congregation was dissolved, and seven years later the site and the surviving buildings were acquired by the Pennsylvania Historical and Museum Commission (PHMC).

THE CLOISTER BECOMES A HISTORIC SITE

The restoration of the buildings started in earnest later in the 1940s, continuing until 1969, when the last of the buildings was completed. During the PHMC's administration of the historic site, work has continued to preserve the buildings and the collection of Cloister artifacts for the purposes of maintaining the record of this unique community and to make it available for visitation by the general public. Specialists in early American music, architecture, material culture, and other disciplines have continued to examine Ephrata to gain understanding of the complexities of thought and behavior of this community. In 1991 a conference held to mark the two-hundredth anniversary of the birth of Conrad Beissel brought leading scholars in many fields to the Cloister to share the results of their latest research and analysis.

Since then, research has progressed primarily underground, through a series of summer archaeological digs. A fascinating yet puzzling find in the summer of 1995 was a large, trumpet-shaped glass tube found deep underground near the site of the *Kedar* building. This object, the only one of its kind ever found in North America, intrigues scholars, who have so far found no references to it in the community's records. Its use, history, and origin are all a matter of guesswork at this point and should continue to be a source of historical intrigue for some time to come.

Other scholars have examined tax and land records, censuses, deeds, wills, and other sorts of public records to glean bits of information about everyday life at the Cloister. Merchants' account books shed light on the interactions between the three groups at Ephrata. Musicologists continue to analyze Ephrata's music, seeking models for it in the works of earlier communities. They dissect the particular harmonization schemes used by the composers and attempt to guess at the vocal techniques that would have produced singing of the form described by Colonial-era visitors.

A final area of research has been a detailed textual analysis of the writings of Beissel and other Cloister members, a task made difficult by the obscurity of these texts and the complex vocabulary and language the writers often employed to express their beliefs. Scholars in this area have also turned to the European antecedents of Ephrata, trying to show the relationship between Ephrata's theology and that expressed by European writers in the Mystic and Pietist tradition. When we learn the extent to which Beissel and his followers were influenced by other thinkers, we will have a better understanding of where and how Ephrata's belief system fits into the main or side currents of European and early American cultural thought.

Peter Miller's Cabin. Miller's death in 1796 precipitated Ephrata's decline. Twenty years later, the last of the celibates died. Miller's cabin is another structure that has not survived. EPHRATA CLOISTER COLLECTION

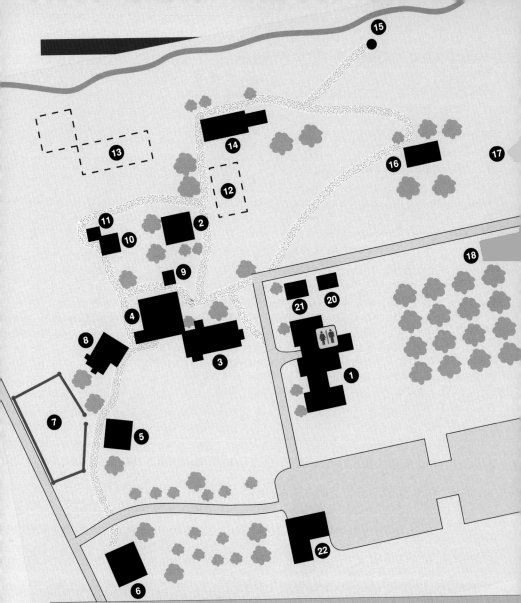

SITE LEGEND

1. Visitor Center
2. Conrad Beissel's House
3. *Saron*, the Sisters' House
4. *Saal*, the Meetinghouse
5. A Weaver's House
6. The Academy
7. God's Acre
8. The Bakery
9. The *Saron* Bake Oven
10. The Physician's House
11. The Small Bake House
12. Site of *Kedar*
13. Site of *Bethania*, the Brothers' House
14. The Printing Office
15. The Cocalico Creek and the Spring
16. The Carpenter's House
17. The Amphitheater
18. The Maintenance Barn*
19. Site of Mount Zion Buildings

Visiting the Site

1 THE VISITOR CENTER

A visit to the Ephrata Cloister begins at the Visitor Center, with the purchase of admission tickets and an orientation to the site. Located here are exhibits, which explain the history, beliefs, and practices of the community, with written documents, hand-crafted original objects, artifacts uncovered in archaeological digs, and many other items. An audiovisual production can be viewed before touring the buildings.

20 The Log Building

21 The Stable

22 Shady Nook Farm

23 The Mount Zion Cemetery

♦♦ Restrooms

* Not open to the public

② CONRAD BEISSEL'S HOUSE

Beissel lived alone in this house for several years, until his death in 1768. Before this, he lived in a variety of places in the community, at times in a larger dormitory, at others in a simple house. He lived simply, accumulating little, as he wrote, studied, and contemplated.

Beissel's meals were delivered from the Brothers' House, which stood about seventy-five paces south of here. In the opposite direction, at that precise distance, stands the Sisters' House. When Israel Acrelius visited Ephrata, he noticed ropes running from this house to the celibates' dormitories. Inquiring, he learned that these ropes were hooked to bells. A clanging in the night meant that Beissel needed everyone to assemble in the Meetinghouse.

The interior walls of this *Fachwerk*, or half-timbered, building have been exposed to display the precision required by this method of construction. Normally these walls would be plastered and whitewashed.

③ *SARON*, THE SISTERS' HOUSE

The Sisters' House is the largest surviving building on the site. Constructed in 1743, this was the home of Ephrata's order of celibate women, formally known as the Roses of Sharon (*Saron* in German). This grand structure has three full floors plus an attic; filled to capacity, it accommodated thirty-six Sisters. Entering *Saron*, the visitor quickly becomes conscious of the low, narrow doors that typify Ephrata. "The gate to heaven is small," lectured Conrad Beissel. *Saron's* doorways, some as low as five feet, show the influence of his teaching upon the building's carpenters. The low doorways were symbolic of the difficulties of the path toward heaven, as taught by Beissel, and remind the visitor today of the importance

placed on suffering by members of the community.

Now furnished to represent the era of the celibate Sisters' residence in the building, *Saron* shows the frugality and austerity of the lives of the original occupants. Its plain white walls, illuminated by light entering through the few small windows, emphasize the sparse furnishings and lack of comfort. The three floors are laid out similarly, each having a central kitchen and small dining room, or refectory; two

large work rooms, one on each side of the kitchen; and approximately twelve small sleeping rooms, where the Sisters took their few hours of rest.

The Sisters were divided into seven groups, called "classes," with each class assigned to a particular work room and a daily occupation. These included spinning, sewing clothes, making *Fraktur*, or tending gardens. As work at Ephrata was thought to be yet another way of praising God, or helping the worker get closer to Him, the act, or process, of the work was more significant than the finished result.

A surviving manuscript known as *The Rose*, or the Sisters' Chronicle, states that the Sisters followed a daily schedule that was strictly regulated by the clock. Arising at 5:00 A.M., they spent an hour in prayer and meditation before beginning work at 6:00. Then, alternating periods of work and prayer, meditation, or contemplation followed until 6:00 P.M., when the only cooked meal of the day was prepared. The Sisters living on each floor used the kitchen to make the simple meal, which

typically consisted of bread, vegetables, fruit, and water. Before eating in the small anteroom or refectory, the Sisters could clear the table by placing objects on the under-top tray, a distinctive feature of Ephrata furniture.

After two hours of instruction in *Fraktur* or music, the Sisters went to their individual sleep-ing rooms at 9:00 P.M. These tiny spaces measured only "four paces by two." The Sisters slept not on beds or cots, but on narrow wooden benches, some as slim as 14 inches, using small wood blocks for pillows. According to Beissel's teachings, comfort could lead to temptation.

After three hours of sleep, at midnight the Sisters awakened and went through the long, narrow passage into their chapel, or *Saal*. Here they held a two-hour prayer service before returning to their rooms and sleeping another three hours. At 5:00 the Ephrata day began anew, echoing the events of the previous day.

 SAAL, THE MEETINGHOUSE

The *Saal*, or the Meeting-house, is one of several chapels that once stood at Ephrata. This one, originally constructed in 1741 for the married Householders, was assigned to the Sisters after they moved into *Saron* four years later. The celibate Broth-ers had a Meetinghouse adjoining their quarters, *Bethania*, much as the *Saal* is connected to *Saron*.

The *Saal* is plain, in keeping with the religious traditions of the Anabaptists and Radical Pietists who inspired Ephrata's belief system. A simple room, with no altar, no crucifix, and minimal ornamentation, shows that at Ephrata a space itself

was not sacred. What was more important for the resi-dents was the individual's progress toward the mystical union with God, aided by the presence of a supportive, like-minded community. Cut off from "the world," in Ephrata the believer was thought to have the best chance to develop spiritually and follow the difficult path toward paradise, the union with God.

The Meetinghouse's shape and dimensions are, however, symbolic. Almost a perfect cube with edges of 40 feet, the *Saal* represented Jerusalem in the minds of Beissel and his followers. The massive central wooden pillar appears to go all the way to the top of the five-story building. Among its few contents are a pair of wooden candlesticks made at Ephrata in the eighteenth century. The Bible that lies on the pulpit table is an old German edition but not the actual book of scripture used here.

On the wall above the pulpit bench, which originally sat in the Brothers' *Saal*, hangs a *Fraktur* reading "God and the virgin lamb must always in us rule, and through eternity not let our faith grow cool," a reminder of the purpose of life at Ephrata. This and the other two large *Frakturs* hanging in the *Saal* are reproductions of originals now hanging in the climate-controlled Visitor Center.

This *Saal* was the place for the Sisters' midnight worship services, and it could also be used for weekly Sabbath observances as well. In later years, this building served as the place of worship for the Householder congregation and its descendant, the German Seventh-Day Baptist Church of Ephrata. In December the Ephrata Cloister Chorus performs here as part of the "Christmas at the Cloister" celebration.

The *Saal* storeroom holds supplies for a love feast or other community activity. Just beyond it is the kitchen, a sandstone addition attached to the building about 1770. In this kitchen, with its large fireplace, the love feast, Ephrata's ceremony of spiritual fellowship, was prepared. The facility also could have served the community as a general-purpose work space. The two-part Dutch door was designed to allow ventilation, by opening the top half while closing the bottom to keep out stray animals.

⑤ A WEAVER'S HOUSE

Before textile mills with water-powered spinning machines and looms were established in America at the end of the eighteenth century, cloth was made at home. Natural fibers, commonly wool or flax, were cleaned and straightened by combing and carding, then stretched and twisted into yarn on a spinning wheel. At Ephrata, spinning was most likely performed by the Sisters, in one of the work rooms in *Saron*. Then skeins of thread were delivered to the weavers, who produced fabric for the community. Ephrata's distinctive garments were made from linen and woolen cloth woven on large hand looms by Brothers who had mastered this skilled craft.

The Weaver's House is an excellent example of the most common house style con-structed by the Pennsylvania Germans. Known as a *Flurküchenhaus,* or "corridor-kitchen house," this dwelling is laid out in the typical Germanic three-room plan. The door opens directly into the *Küche,* or kitchen, with its characteristic central raised-hearth fireplace and chimney. The hearth is elevated not only for convenience but also as a safety measure: Dangling clothes were less likely to contact hot embers than if the hearth was even with the floor.

The most important room of the house is the *Stube,* or stove room, which backs up to the fireplace. Frequently these rooms held iron or ceramic stoves, into which hot coals were placed through an opening in the fireplace back. The *Stube* was the location for work, meals, study, and many other daily activities. Because few early settlers owned chairs, benches built directly into the walls of the house served as seats. The third room, or *Kammer,* could have been used as a bedroom or as additional work space.

⑥ THE ACADEMY

Constructed in 1837, the Academy was a private boarding and day school operated by the German Seventh-Day Baptist Church. It had a pre-college curriculum for young men and women, offering such subjects as geography, algebra, natural philosophy, and chemistry. Because there were few public high schools in rural Pennsylvania at this time, academies such as Ephrata's flourished. According to a notice in a Lancaster newspaper, the school was located in "one of the most healthy and moral sections" of the county.

After the Civil War, the building was leased by Ephrata Township and used as a public grade school. This arrangement lasted until the 1920s.

The Academy represents a long tradition of interest in education at Ephrata. In 1740 the first school opened here, and both elementary and classical schools were conducted in the community.

The Ephrata Cloister library and archives are located on the second floor of the Academy. The site's collection of books, original documents and imprints on microfilm, and files on Ephrata individuals and families are available for use by genealogists and researchers by appointment.

7 GOD'S ACRE

God's Acre is believed to be Ephrata's second graveyard. Most of the individuals interred here were members or descendants of the Householder congregation, but several celibates were buried here as well. Chief among these was Conrad Beissel, founder and guiding spirit of Ephrata, who died in 1768. Beside Beissel's grave lies that of his successor, Peter Miller, the one-time Reformed minister who lived at Ephrata for nearly sixty years. A quaint memorial to Dietrich and Margarethe Fahnestock, a prominent Householder couple, sits near the cemetery's entrance. Many of the old marble stones are so weathered that their inscriptions are practically illegible.

8 THE BAKERY

Made of stone and built into the side of a hill, the Bakery is reminiscent of bank-type homes from Switzerland. On the ground floor are two "squirrel tail" ovens, one attached to the rear and one to the right side of the large fireplace. To heat the ovens, the Brothers of the bakery crew built roaring fires directly inside them. Meanwhile, the loaves of raw dough were waiting in the rising room. Once the fire was

reduced to hot embers, the ovens, now hot enough, were scraped clean. Then, like clockwork, the loaves were passed through the opening in the rising room door, placed on the bakers' flat, long-handled peels, and placed in the ovens to bake. The heat was reflected from the beehive-shaped ceiling and walls.

Water for the bakery came from the simple wooden pump at the top of the stone steps. Several strokes of the handle filled a bucket, then its contents were hurled into the chute jutting out from the wall behind. Gravity did the rest.

The Bakery's upper floor may have been a work area, a center where food and cloth-ing were distributed to the poor, or a storage area. It is also possible that several widows from the Householder group may have dwelled here at some time. From this spot so close to *Saron* they would have been able to join the Sisters in their daily activities and continue their involvement in life at Ephrata.

❾ THE *SARON* BAKE OVEN

This small, free-standing oven was built in the early nineteenth century. The red clay roof tiles were common on Pennsylvania German out-buildings of the period. To pro-duce the curved shape of the ridge tiles, damp clay was formed over the tile maker's thigh prior to firing. The flatter tiles were formed in a mold.

 THE PHYSICIAN'S HOUSE

Over the years, a number of men associated with the Ephrata community filled the role of physician for the settlement. There were no medical schools in the colonies until 1765, when the University of Pennsylvania opened the first one, and few American doctors held degrees from European institutions. Almost 90 percent of Colonial doctors learned their craft by apprenticing with practicing physicians.

The eighteenth century was the era of "heroic medicine," when bleeding and purging were standard treatments for many ailments. Most medicines were derived from plants, and the physician usually functioned as a pharmacist, too. Herbs and other plants used to make medicines were grown in Ephrata's gardens.

The Physician's House represents typical early Pennsylvania German architecture. A prominent interior feature is the cast-iron five-plate stove, which heated the *Stube*, or stove room. The stove was fed by placing embers into it from the fireplace in the *Küche* (kitchen) through an opening in the dividing wall. This stove is dated from 1765 and was made by Samuel Flowers, an iron master from Berks County.

THE SMALL BAKE HOUSE
To the rear of the Physician's House sits another bake oven, offering evidence once again of the importance of bread to the community. Currently this building gets occasional use as the site of craft demonstrations in summer or on special occasions.

 SITE OF *KEDAR*

An example of a "missing" part of Ephrata history can be found in the grassy expanse that stretches between the Stable, the Beissel House, the Print Shop, and the Carpenter's House. Intensive archaeological work conducted at this spot has unearthed the foundations of two major buildings, described in sources but never seen by modern eyes. The first foundation, rectangular in shape with dimensions closely paralleling *Saron,* may be the base of *Kedar,* Ephrata's first communal building. Nearby, situated at an angle to the first foundation, is a stone footing that may have supported the earliest house of worship, known as the *Bethaus*. These buildings date from the first days of the Ephrata community. While the *Bethaus* was dismantled only four years after it was built, evidence suggests that *Kedar* survived until the early nineteenth century.

 SITE OF *BETHANIA*, THE BROTHERS' HOUSE

Built in 1746, as the Brothers left the heights of Mount Zion to remove to the meadow where other community buildings lay, *Bethania* contained sleeping rooms, kitchens, refectories, and work spaces similar to those in the Sisters' House. It had an adjoining Meetinghouse similar to *Saron's Saal*. Because of deterioration, the Brothers' House was dismantled in the early twentieth century.

THE PRINTING OFFICE

When Ephrata's first press arrived from Frankfurt, Germany, in 1743, it was probably housed in the Brothers' House on Mount Zion. Then after *Bethania* was constructed, it is likely that the press was situated there. The press in this building dates from the nineteenth century but is operated in much the same manner as the older one. Displayed in the type case are pieces of German lead type that were unearthed during an archaeological excavation at *Bethania* site in 1965.

This building was constructed in two stages. The older, west end dates from 1735 and may be one of the oldest historic structures on the site. The east end, built nearly a century later, shows a marked departure from the early Ephrata style of construction.

THE COCALICO CREEK AND THE SPRING

New members of the Ephrata community were baptized in the Cocalico Creek. The creek's currents also powered the Brothers' sawmill, gristmill, linseed oil mill, fulling mill (used to process cloth), and two paper mills. The spring was one of the early water supplies for the Ephrata community.

16 THE CARPENTER'S HOUSE

A delightful little building set apart from the others is the Carpenter's House, located along the rise known as Mount Zion. When Beissel and his first followers came to the site that became Ephrata, they lived in small dwellings of this type. Solitaries were celibates, lone individuals who had forsaken all earthly comfort to follow the life of suffering advocated by Beissel. After the construction of the large community buildings, some individuals preferred to remain in isolated homes of this type.

Brothers Sealthiel (Sigmund Landent) and Kenan (Jacob Funk) were master carpenters who directed the construction of buildings and crafted furniture for the community.

18 THE MAINTENANCE BARN

The Maintenance Barn, which is not open to the public, is a twentieth-century structure constructed to resemble Ephrata's original buildings. The orchard near the barn replicates one that flourished at the Cloister in the eighteenth century and caught the attention of many visitors to the community. As fruits and vegetables made up major portions of the Ephrata diet, the orchard's importance can hardly be overstated.

SITE OF THE MOUNT ZION BUILDINGS

Mount Zion was the site of several early structures occupied by the Brothers, including the building used as a hospital for Continental soldiers in the winter of 1777. Recent archaeological projects are giving more clues about the location, sizes, and uses of these buildings.

THE LOG BUILDING

This small eighteenth-century barn, of typical Pennsylvania German design, was removed during the construction of the Pennsylvania Turnpike in the 1940s and brought to the Cloister. It is now used for special activities and displays.

THE STABLE

This stable is a reproduction of the original structure that stood on this spot. It housed the few horses and cows kept by the community. Now it holds a collection of eighteenth-century farm equipment, such as a plow, a harrow, grain cradles, and rakes. The large feed trough is from an old Lancaster County barn.

SHADY NOOK FARM

Some of the last members of the German Seventh-Day Baptist Church of Ephrata lived near the historic buildings on the site at Shady Nook Farm. Although the farmhouse, which stood near the Visitor Center, has been razed, the barn remains. It houses the Museum Store at Ephrata Cloister, which carries a comprehensive selection of books and reproductions of Ephrata *Fraktur*. Authentic handicrafts, recordings by the Cloister Chorus, and many other mementos are also available. Proceeds from the store fund the many educational and cultural activities presented by the Ephrata Cloister Associates throughout the year.

MOUNT ZION CEMETERY

The most prominent feature of the Mount Zion Cemetery is the obelisk honoring the Revolutionary War soldiers who died at Ephrata in 1777 and 1778. A number of early members of the Ephrata community are also buried here.

For information on hours, tours, programs, and activities at the Ephrata Cloister, visit **www.phmc.state.pa.us.**

Further Reading

Alderfer, E. G. *The Ephrata Commune: An Early American Counterculture*. Pittsburgh: University of Pittsburgh Press, 1985.

Bradley, John. "Pushing William Penn's 'Holy Experiment' to Its Limits: Ephrata Cloister," *Pennsylvania Heritage* 22 (fall 1996): 14–23.

Coleman, John M., Robert G. Crist, and John B. Frantz, eds. *Pennsylvania's Religious Leaders*. University Park, Pa.: Pennsylvania Historical Association, 1986.

Kelly, Joseph J., Jr. *Pennsylvania: The Colonial Years, 1681–1776*. Garden City, N.Y.: Doubleday & Company, 1980.

Lamech and Agrippa. *Chronicon Ephratense: A History of the Community of the Seventh Day Baptists at Ephrata*. New York: Lenox Hill Publishing, 1972.

Reichmann, Felix, and Eugene E. Doll. *Ephrata as Seen by Contemporaries*. Allentown, Pa.: Pennsylvania German Folklore Society, 1953.

Sangmeister, Ezechial. *Life and Conduct (Leben und Wandel)*. Ephrata, Pa.: Historical Society of the Cocalico Valley, 1986.

Schwartz, Sally. *"A Mixed Multitude": The Struggle for Toleration in Colonial Pennsylvania*. New York: New York University Press, 1987.

Warfel, Stephen G. *Historical Archaeology at Ephrata Cloister*. Harrisburg, Pa.: Pennsylvania Historical and Museum Commission, 1994–1999.

Weiser, Frederick S., and Howell J. Heaney. *The Pennsylvania German Fraktur of the Free Library of Philadelphia*. Breinigsville, Pa.: Pennsylvania German Society, 1976.

Yoder, Don, Vernon Gunnion and Carol J. Hopf. *Pennsylvania German Fraktur and Color Drawings*. Lancaster, Pa.: Landis Valley Associates, 1969.